ETHIOPIAN VIGNETTES

SEEING IS BELIEVING

JAMES MURREN

Introduction

My wife and I lived and worked in Ethiopia for six months in 2005 and again in 2008 for a month. This great opportunity came about from the generosity of Mr. Harry Stokes, the visionary leader behind a global household energy revolution called Project Gaia. During our seven months there, we worked and traveled non-stop, seeing many far-off places that few people who visit Ethiopia will ever see. I am grateful.

What are offered in these pages are my observations and understandings of Ethiopia at that time. I have also included photos because I believe they can enhance the reader's experience. To be sure, my words are only one person's interpretation of the lands and lives of Africa's horn that were experienced by a foreigner in a moment of time. Additionally, this collection of writings is not, by any means, a concrete statement.

From the magical mystery that is Lalibela, the heart-break that exists in Somali and Eritrean refugee camps, the day-to-day goings-on in Addis Ababa to the long-distance runners of Ethiopia and the bumpy road to democratization, I share with you my sincere attempt at providing a glimpse into the homeland of the diverse peoples that I grew to greatly respect and admire.

To learn more about Project Gaia, go to:
www.projectgaia.com

To learn more about The Denan Project, go to:
www.thedenanproject.com

Please consider making a donation to either/both projects. If you wish to specifically support their efforts in Ethiopia, note it on your contribution. Fifty-percent of final profits from sales of this book will go to support Project Gaia's refugee program in Ethiopia.

*Writings in this book from 2005 first appeared as a bi-weekly column in my hometown newspaper, <u>The Evening Sun</u>, Hanover, PA.

"Some Aloe Vera, Vitamins, and a Lot of Prayer"

We arrived in Addis Ababa ("New Flower" in Amharic) around 7:15 p.m. local time after 15 hours on the plane. Tired to the bones, we were picked up at the airport and carried off to our new home in northeast "Addis," how Ethiopians call their capital city.

A welcoming dinner was in order at a local Italian restaurant. Despite wanting to crash into bed, we joined our new co-workers and host-country nationals with sincere smiles and a new-found energy reserve.

Plates of good pasta and Ethiopian Gouder red wine filled our stomachs when we finally laid down to sleep somewhere around 11:30 p.m.

****

Saturday, the ninth of July, 2005. We accompanied our fellow project members to a stove demonstration at one of the Missionaries of Charity's (Mother Teresa's sisters) orphanages. A few hours before our early afternoon arrival, the sisters had come out of an eight day silent retreat. When we walked in, they were ready for the demo, talkative, and quite lively!

The demo went well. They were receptive to the stoves, asked excellent questions, gave experienced suggestions, and exuded a simplicity I have only yearned for, having never truly lived it. Before departing, they each carried a stove and fuel to take back with them to their homes and other orphanages located across the city.

My wife asked Sister Mercy if we could see the orphanage; it was one that cared specifically for those inflicted with HIV/AIDS. She was very inviting, allowing us to go with two Irish women volunteering at the orphanage, along with our co-workers. We first visited the room of children in the gravest of health. They had little time left to live, a couple of months at most. Death lived among the dying. One child was hooked to an IV. The others lay in cribs while a nanny looked after their needs.

We moved on to the girls' living quarters. Happy, laughing, and playing, I was struck by the innocence and zest for life that emanated from their beings. Reaching out their hands, they wanted to hold our hands as we walked through their home, their play areas. I was not able to recall ever holding the hand of someone who I knew was going to die in the near future, possibly before I will leave Africa. Helpless.

The boys' rooms were next on our visit. We entered the first room and were greeted by some 50 boys, aged 4-9, though they looked maybe 2-5 years old. They sang for us a spiritual song in their native tongue. I wanted to cry.

Why was I feeling so sad in the presence of such beauty? I wish I could have sung along with them. Their singing voices were strong, and their eyes big and round. Life thrived.

Moving on, we commented on how clean and orderly the orphanage was. In fact, it was spotless! Each room was bright and warm, with paintings of animals and Biblical scenes on the walls.

×**

A social worker at the orphanage told us that treatment for the children consists of "aloe vera [for the skin lesions], vitamins, and a lot of prayer." He was proud to point out that they grow their own aloe at the orphanage, the spiky plants sticking out from a small hillside.

No medication or drugs are available for the children. They are too expensive, and not available. Therefore, the Sisters and those who work at the orphanage do what they can to provide the children with an environment that gives them their dignity while dying. They lessen the suffering and increase the love.

****

Meanwhile, right now in pharmaceutical offices in the West, people work to protect their patents and rights to the production of Anti-Retro Viral drugs. They maintain high prices to make a profit on their technology, fooling themselves by thinking they are doing good deeds by advancing medicine when what they are really doing is advancing death by keeping the medicine from the sickest of the sick. Is human health care a service or is it a business? When did it become the norm to make a profit off of humanity's illnesses?

(written 24 July 2005)

Kite Flying
Under a July Ethiopian Sky

I remember reading somewhere that the children of Afghanistan were not allowed to fly kites under the Taliban. The sky was devoid of bright diamond and box-shaped colors attached to strings fluttering in the wind.

In Honduras, watching boys run down the main road of my village with kites made of thrown-away plastic and paper always brought a smile to my face.

Kite-flying is an innocent activity that eases the flyer's mood, usually giving him/her a sense of in-the-moment joy and happiness no matter the age.

Why would anyone ban kite flying?

****

After two weeks in Addis, our Ethiopian co-workers' invitation to see the Rift Valley Lakes region situated along the main hard road heading south out of the city was welcomed into my ears and transferred throughout my body with much needing-to-get-out-of-the-city enthusiasm.

We departed Friday morning on the 22nd day of July around nine in the morning. The weather was looking good; rainless on a typically rainy morning of the rainy season. An hour of twisting-and-turning and stopping-and-going through Addis' morning traffic, and we finally made it into the countryside where farmers worked dark-soiled fields with oxen and wooden plows with metal blades. The planting season was upon them. A sunny blue sky pockmarked with white clouds shined above all of us.

A scheduled itinerary was not in our pockets. We rolled down the road, stopping for a late breakfast and sun-worshipping from our morning meal outdoor seats.

Eventually, sometime in the early afternoon we pulled off the hard road and bumped our way to Lake Langano. Though safe for swimming, I opted to sit back and take in the naturally-occurring brown lake laid out before me. Eggs digesting and shade from an acacia tree stretched above me, I was in one of those be-here-now modes. My wife beside me was the Zen center.

****

By evening we reached Lake Awasa sitting about an hour or so more down the road. We secured rooms at a local hotel in town, had a drink thirty minutes later while listening to crickets and slapping mosquitoes by the water, and capped the night with plates of Western-style prepared beef and chicken.

The next morning we headed to the hot springs of Wondo Genet. To arrive there, we had to bump again along a dirt road. Villages and lone thatch-roofed, mud-walled houses were scattered along the way, with a couple of major towns plopped down here and there. People walked and some bounced on two-wheeled trailers pulled by donkeys and horses as we drove by in our mini-bus. On this road, unlike anywhere I had been in Honduras, the road was well-traveled by moving people. In Honduras, most times I saw people sitting by the road waiting for a ride. They did not walk.

Outside my window, I saw human beings of all ages wearing what some would call rags. Distended stomachs on toddlers sneaked out from undersized dirty shirts. Women and girls carried jugs of water and bundles of firewood with tired faces. Men walked behind cattle and rode the two-wheeled trailers laughing and under what appeared to be minimal-to-no physical stress.

When will our world recognize the plight of women? If we are to "assist," "provide aid for," "save," "help" the less fortunate of our world, wouldn't a good place to start be: getting girls out of the home and free from the guise of cultural norms and into the classroom?

****

We opted to not swim in the main swimming pools at the hot springs "resort." They were too crowded with Addis weekenders on holiday. Instead, we walked up the mountain behind the pool area hoping to see some monkeys while taking in a little nature.

Passing by the very hot stream (locals cook corn and potatoes in it) that fed the pools below we made our way into a beautiful pine forest, a reforestation project facilitated by a nearby forestry school. Mountains over nine thousand feet high surrounded us on a bright afternoon. A troop of black and white colobus monkeys suddenly appeared, jumping through the trees above us.

Oh, the marvel of watching primates fly through the sky from tree to tree!

****

The following day, Sunday, we stopped off at Lake Abiata-Shala National Park on our way back to Addis. Ostriches greeted us at the park's entrance, the site quickly enhanced by a single gazelle galloping through the grass in front of us. We were set on going to the lake's shore to see the colony of flamingos that live on the silver body of water.

Again, we were bouncing along a dirt road in good spirits. Children approached our vehicle asking for pens, money, etc. as our mini-bus slowed to get through the mud holes and broken sections of the road. When we picked up speed, the children did not stay behind. They ran beside us for minutes at a time, persistent and with warm smiles on their faces. They never seemed to tire. Mostly boys, as the girls were probably off tending to house needs, they waited for us to slow down and then came up to our windows asking for us to give them something. We would speed up, and so would they. Some of them followed us for the half hour ride down to the beach.

×*********

What is one to do when "poor" children run beside one's car asking for so little? Does one contribute to this reality by handing a pen or coins out the window? What does one teach by doing this? What do the children learn? Does this energy and persistence of the children manage its way through older society? Does one pass things out the window knowing it very likely will lead the children to fight over possessing it? Does one pass things out the window knowing that it will undoubtedly encourage more kids to continue running?

****

I unfurled the kite when we hit the beach. Rainbow colors immediately blazed in the sun-filled sky. My personal solidarity gesture with the spirit again living amongst Afghanistan's children was ever-present in the reaction of everyone on the beach: Ethiopians, Americans and the Irish. Turns holding the string and sharing of the binoculars to view the flamingos occupied our time.

We could not approach the water's edge. The beach was very muddy and required rubber boots. That did not matter much to us. We were as happy as kite flyers with the sponge-like beach below our soles. We literally jumped up and down on sand that reacted the way Jell-o does when pressed on.

Jell-o jumping and a kite in the sky. Didn't the mystical Jesus say something about entering heaven when we find the child in us?

(written 31 July 2005)

On the road to Awasa, Ethiopia

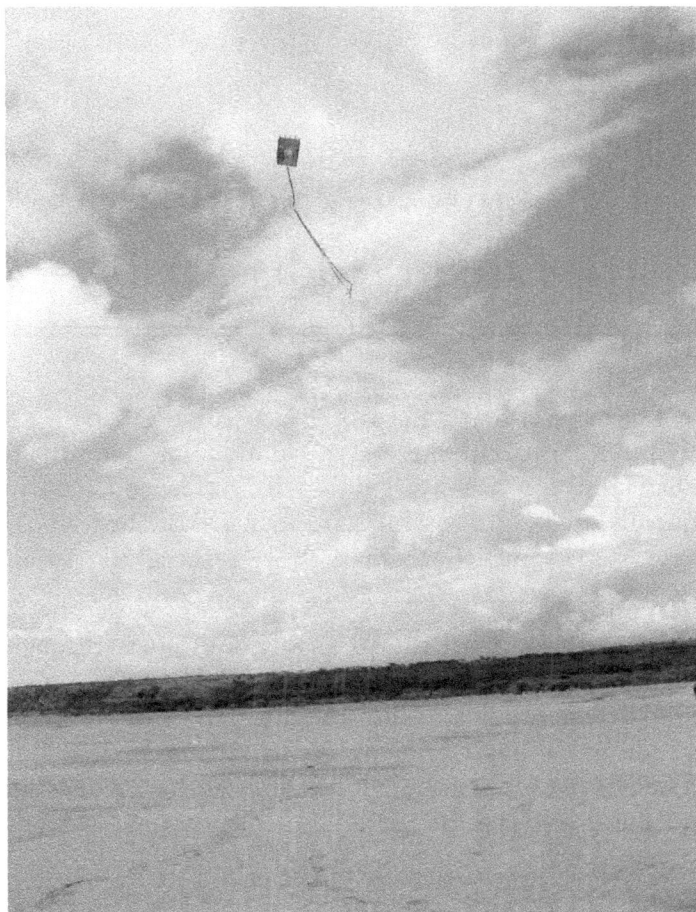

Sights and Sounds
of Life in Addis Ababa

We have been living and working in Addis Ababa for a month. Like all cities, there are sights, sounds and other characteristics that are specific to Addis and, consequently, make it a city like no other. I thought I would take some time to share with you some of Addis' uniqueness.

Boys and men herd sheep, mostly, and goats through the streets in search of green space to fatten them up a little before heading to the slaughter yard. It is common to see the animals bringing traffic to a stop. It is uncommon to see anyone get upset about having to stop for the sheep. It is life here.

****

We came to a traffic circle when the traffic policeman dressed in a khaki uniform brought all cars to a halt. Across the way four men scooted and crawled to the other side of the road. They were obviously people who lived on the streets, begging to exist.

Why were they crawling and scooting? They couldn't walk. Victims of polio? Birth defects? War's wounded? Not a single horn blared. I am certain that I felt a sense of compassion emanating from the cars.

****

Meskal Square in the morning is filled with runners. Calisthenics are the activity when we drive by on our way to work. High-stepping in groups that keep a uniform circle seem to be the standard warm-up. Ethiopia is world-renowned for its long-distance runners. Many a New York, Boston and Olympic marathon participant has run in the Square. In the evening when we drive by on our way home from work, people are running in the square as well.

****

"Mini-confusion" is the local name of an intersection that operates in ordered chaos. Cars and buses manage to get through it without incident. There are no traffic lights. In fact, when lights were introduced, it apparently caused more confusion. In general, driving in the city somehow has few accidents, as far as I have seen. But, when I sit in the passenger's seat, I sometimes slam my foot to the floor in search of the brake that doesn't exist. Yet, as time has gone by, I have come to realize that there is an order to the driving patterns in the city. Basically, it is a system that operates on good will and kindness. Road rage has not arrived in Addis. Drivers wave each other around and through the traffic. Also, a beep of the horn signals walkers to step aside a little, and they do.

****

Women sit by the road with ears of corn cooking on a charcoal stove. Men stop and buy an ear and eat it. Instead of biting the kernels off, they pull them off in a rubbing motion that seems more efficient than biting. After they have a handful, they toss them into their mouths like popcorn.

****

Shanty towns with homes that have roofs made from scrapped metal gleam in the sunshine. In the background you can see a few tall buildings that mark "modernization" and "progress." There's even a glass high-rise office building being built near Meskal Square.

****

Blue and white mini-buses that transport people around the city all have a young man that hollers the route for his bus out of the sliding door window. It is not just his head that hangs out of the window; it is his whole upper torso. One route-caller was going down the road holding an umbrella in the rain as he extended his body out of the window.

****

"Ferangi" is what the children sometimes call out from their doorsteps when we walk by them on the streets. "Foreigner" denotes that we do not look like them. They almost always say it with a smile on their faces.

****

Every morning around six we hear prayers in the distance. They are being said in Amharic over a loud speaker at the Christian Orthodox church that sits up the hill behind our house. They only last a few minutes. I think of how this would never happen back home. There would certainly be an ordinance against it. I was told that when a new bishop took up residence in Arat Kilo, a section of the city near our house, he had one of his churches turn down the loud speaker. It was waking him earlier than he liked!

****

Up by Addis Ababa University there are lots of students on the streets. There is a good energy there. I like being around young people that are full of ideas, passion, and excitement. Well-dressed, they do not follow the relaxed fashion found on America's campuses.

****

Cafes that serve fine pastries and excellent cups of coffee and tea are found throughout Addis, a holdover of when the Italians were here. Coffee originates in Ethiopia and is the favorite, but tea does hold its ground as a beverage of choice. Macchiatos seem to be everyone's favorite though, a quick blast of caffeine and calcium.

****

Addis is a city with a village-like feel to it. Friends and family stop to greet each other on the streets, giving a hearty hug and a genuine smile. They really are happy to stop and say "hello." The animals certainly give the city a rural feel. Meanwhile, sprawling neighborhoods and the newer, taller buildings give Addis its "city" status.

Though it has only been thirty days that we have been here, Addis feels like a welcoming place to me. I have been able to ease my way into life with relatively no difficulty. Addis Ababa is treating me well.

(written 7 August 2005)

Ethiopia's Runners, Among the World's Elite Athletes

Our introduction to Ethiopia's running elite occurred happenstance. My wife was coming out of an elevator at a local hotel/restaurant when Ethiopia's, and arguable the world's, greatest male runner entered the other elevator. She had a sighting of Kenenisa Bekele, but would not have known he was anybody or someone famous had our Ethiopian co-workers not have been so excited and wide-eyed when they saw him.

"Do you know who that is…that's Kenenisa Bekele…he beat Gabreselassie at the Olympics."

Gabreselassie? That would be THE Haile Gabreselassie, one of the greatest long-distance runners to ever lace up a pair of running shoes, and compatriot to Kenenisa. Haile's name is known throughout every household in Ethiopia, and Kenenisa is fast becoming Haile's heir.

****

Last weekend, the 2005 World Championships in Athletics came to a close after nine days of competition in Helsinki, Finland. Ethiopia sported a field of contenders that was expected to do very well in the long-distance races. I doubt if anyone in the land of "13

Months of Sunshine" expected their hopefuls to run their way to the top of world's running elite.

A quick recap of the week's events follows:

In the Men's 10,000 meter race, it was Bekele taking gold with fellow Ethiopian Sihine bringing home the silver. The two separated from the pack by turn two of the final lap and sprinted against each other to the finish line, Kenenisa winning comfortably.

In the Women's 10,000 meter, Ethiopia swept the medal stands. Tirunesh Dibaba won gold, followed by Adere, and Dibaba's sister, Ejegayehu, winning the bronze. Even more impressive, in the Women's 5000 meter, Ethiopia finished in the top four spots. Dibaba won gold again, followed by Meseret Defar, Ejegayehu with another bronze and Meselech Melkamu rounding out the foursome.

For Tirunesh Dibaba, winning the 5000 was an historic moment. She was the first woman to ever win the 5000 and 10,000 meter races in the same competition.

Not to forget the Men's 5000 meter race, it was Sihine again winning a silver medal while Bekele watched from the sidelines due to an injury.

****

All week long, Addis was abuzz over the results coming out of Helsinki. TVs in stores were set to the games. Crowds stood and watched, men and women alike. You could feel the pride, despite the natural resolve of Ethiopian shyness and reticence. Ethiopians would never say "we are the best" or "we kicked their…" I like to believe that they know it, but do not have to flaunt it. They may think such things in their private thoughts, but to verbalize it…well, that would not be how things are done in Ethiopia.

However, they do celebrate!

We were on our way home from work when we got caught up in a traffic jam on Debre Zeit Road by Meskal Square. We could see some people running towards the National Stadium, and then horns started honking and blaring. The runners, Ethiopia's heroes, were being paraded through town from Bole International Airport.

Inside the stadium, dignitaries said some words, the runners were showered with flowers and praise, and the people of Ethiopia filled the stands and cheered as their winners were introduced to them. The sun was shining out from behind the rain clouds. A honey golden hue kissed the downtown area.

And those dignitaries...those politicos, using the moment to look good. However, the Ethiopian people would have nothing of it. They yelled and screamed to drown out the words of the men recognizing an opportune time when they saw one. Remembering the thirty-six students gunned down in a peaceful protest of election results a few months back, the people were again protesting with their yells and screams. Except this time they were expressing the emotion of: let us enjoy this moment for what it is, which is not a political moment.

The tension subsided, and after more accolades, Bekele and Dibaba were interviewed for the crowd to hear. Roars and smiles in response to their responses, a few camera flashes, the flying of Ethiopian flags, and that warm golden sun after the early afternoon downpours had me feeling that Ethiopia was the center of the universe, if only for a short time and in the hearts of a few thousand people.

(written 21 August 2005)

Journal Entry, 23 August 2005, Addis Ababa

It did not rain today…seems the rainy season is winding down. Days are getting warmer, which I am wholeheartedly welcoming…hoping the warm sun will dry out this chest cold I've been dealing with for a week or so now. Speaking of rain, when it rains, it pours here. It doesn't know how to have a good ol' farmer's rain.

Heading out to UNHCR Shimelba camp in the morning. Am looking forward to experiencing Tigray people and gaining some insight into the region…hope to talk with Dr. Amare about the history of northern Ethiopia and Eritrea. Will be nice to get out of the office, and Addis.

Sometimes is difficult to keep the perspective of the people—who we really work for—when banging away at a keyboard and filing reports. Working in the field and talking with the people about the stoves, their lives, sharing time with them is what I need at this point in the project.

Finished reading Thiongo's "Petals of Blood." He is fast becoming one of my favorite writers. Blows my mind = the creativity in which he sets up his explosive and powerful critiques of humanity.

"Devil on the Cross" and now "Petals." Need to find more of his writings…will check out the African's Bookstore over in Piazza to see if I can find a used copy.

It is very quiet here in our home. I like the quiet.

Mornings are not as nice. The daily barrage of prayers over the loudspeaker at the church up on the hill has lost all novelty, cultural interest, whatever you care to call it. It wakes me up before my body is ready to wake. I find it an invasion of my space…maybe more my mind. I plot out how I am going to walk up there one night and cut the cord. Though I suspect there is a guard and that it would be bad for relations, etc!!

Anyway…

Next week I'll turn 31. Not sure what that means. Or how I am supposed to feel about it. I like what I am doing and where I am, so I guess I am supposed to be doing what I am doing at this age.

I miss my mountain bike immensely. Seriously, it is absurd how much time I spend thinking about my bike and riding. It's been a nuisance, this missing being on the trail thing, bombing down a forest road, rock-hopping, jonesin' on singletrack dreams…maybe when I start popping the malaria meds I will have a lucid mtbing dream that will cure me of this illness.

I am tired. The instant mashed taters sit in my gut like a water balloon.

This land they call Ethiopia…I am coming to know, and like what I am coming to know…its people so kind and so warm, make me feel at home in my skin…oh Axum, I cannot wait till you reveal your wonder to me…will I get a little insight on Thursday night…and those mountains "the roof of Africa"…I yearn to look out over you and feel your high altitude breezes…absorb me in your existence Simien, and I will beg of you no more.

Wow! Not sure where that came from.

I wish I could speak Amharic. Language opens worlds.

The evening is getting late, and I need my rest. Will be nice to start a new book tonight. Soyinka's "Ake" is on the reading docket. Only a few weeks until we'll be in his land, Nigeria. West Africa…land of big drums, and home to slave castles and the building of America's dream found in the bones scattered across the Atlantic's floor. What better way to understand my country's foundation than through walking and talking on the shores that my history books forgot to tell me about.

Feeling angry now.

Ok, think of the children celebrating the holy day the other evening. Voices singing in the night. Sticks banging against the ground. Rattles shaking in their hands. A big moon up in the sky.

Children singing, is there anything more beautiful this world can offer?

Happy. Again.

l-i-f-e, LIFE, in a Refugee Camp in Northern Ethiopia

"Before the CleanCook Stove, I would gather fuelwood one time each week with my camel. It would take four hours. I still gather wood, but only one camel load every two weeks...I hide when I gather wood, and if the militia gets me, they take my wood. Sometimes they come into the camp and take the wood. And politics is a part of it, because we are Eritreans. I have had stones thrown at me. When I've been alone gathering wood and they have found me, I have been hit by them." — Senie Senie lives in the United Nations High Commissioner for Refugees (UNHCR) Shimelba camp along the Ethiopia/Eritrea border in northwestern Ethiopia. She, like tens of thousands of other Eritreans, has fled her homeland in fear for her life, as anyone aged 16-50, male and female, is likely to be forced into a government-dictated military that has a history of attacking its neighbors to the endpoint of needless deaths for tens of thousands of Eritreans.

Senie has the added burden of being Kunama, a minority ethnicity that survives on the lower rungs of Eritrea's socioeconomic ladder.

I shared thirty minutes or so of life with her and her husband while collecting narratives that focused on their use of our stove and its effects on their lives. Her experience of gathering wood to cook her family's meals is commonplace in the Shimelba camp, and in many camps throughout Africa.

There exists a daily competition for local natural resources between refugee communities and local communities. Scholars call the violence stemming from this competition "environmental conflict." The issues are complex, never having one solution, and often lead to the playing out of the ugly side of our humanity. An example of the complexity is Senie's remark of being Eritrean as one of the causes for the problems she experiences while fuelwood gathering.

Is the competition for wood strictly "environmental?" What place does nationality and recent history between Eritrea and Ethiopia have in the assessment, as 5-6 years ago the two countries were engaged in Africa's bloodiest war at the time?

While in the camp, my wife and I interviewed sixteen families that have been using our project's ethanol-fueled stove (the CleanCook Stove). Almost everyone spoke of spending several days a week for up to 6-10 hours a day walking, searching for and gathering wood for cooking on their traditional three-stone open-fire stove before receiving the CleanCook. Physical pain and aching tiredness from carrying the wood loads on their backs was expressed by all of the women, as they are the primary fuelwood gatherers. Senie is fortunate in this manner; she has a camel to carry her wood, a rarity amongst Kunama fuelwood gatherers.

The local militia permits the gathering of downed wood only. Trees are not to be cut. If ax marks are found on the wood, the wood is confiscated. If the gatherers have money, they can pay the militia to keep the wood, an illegal act sometimes practiced by the militia. We had one woman who attested to handing over money for her wood.

****

When we landed on the grass airstrip on the outskirts of Shire, I knew my time in Ethiopia's remote north was something I had needed for a while. When I hopped into the UN Land Cruiser and found myself in the back seat meandering for an hour and half in a northerly direction towards the outpost town of Sheraro, the needing dissipated.

Endless vistas of rain-fed green landscape and a winding dirt road scattered with men walking on the sides with their camels and donkeys and AK-47s strapped over their shoulders forced me to live travel's greatest addiction: trying to grasp relative existence. What does the man of Tigray think while walking? Why the gun on the shoulder? Hunting? Protection?

Is this the far boundaries of the "Middle East," with the camels and the mosque minarets on the horizon?

****

To be a refugee is one of life's most sorrowful states of existence. You are not safe in your homeland. Maybe you are not welcomed there. So you flee. You try to make a place for you and your family in a new land where you are not welcomed either.

All the while you dream of returning to your native place, to bring alive your memories of the winds blowing through the trees in front of your home, the taste of food grown in the soils you crumpled in your hands as a child, the kisses received from faces of your loved ones, your neighbors.

If you are not dreaming of returning, you dream of going to America or Europe, asking the folks in charge of your resettlement what the status of your case is from one week to the next. You try to find peace and belonging with your fellow refugees, but deep down you are alone and you are yearning for normalcy.

Yet, in the camp, we were reminded of the strength and resilience of our collective humanity. An offering of a seat and a cup of tea and some bread while we talked taught us the gift of kindness. An open door to join them in their mud-walled houses taught us the lesson of hospitality. Offering to cut some beautiful red and orange flowers from the garden along their fencerow for us to bring back to put on our table in Addis taught us the definition of giving.

Why is it that those with so little find a way to make it seem that they have so much, enough to always have something to give? Why does it feel so good to be in their presence? How is it that they never run out of smiles to give? Or, are the smiles for folks like me, visitors? But I have seen them greet each other...the smiles are for everyone, I believe.

****

Senie will go to gather wood this week to bake injera, a kind of bread that is the staple for all foods here in Ethiopia. The Clean Cook Stove is not preferred for baking injera, as baking injera requires a large pan that will not properly fit on the stove, not yet anyway. Most likely she will feel much anxiety as she walks out from her door in the pre-dawn hours of the morning to get a head start on the day's heat. Will the local militia cause problems for her?

I hope with every bit I can muster that she will not be hit by stones, bitten by a snake, chased by hyenas, struck by militia fists, have her womanhood violated, will not have to pay for her legally gathered wood...that she can return to her home with her camel load of wood and can sit down and bake her *injera*.

That she can eat *shero wot* in peace with her husband. That her neighbors will stop and say hello and that their voices will carry together into the warm night. That she will feel that feeling of belonging to a place, if only for a brief moment, and that in that moment she can look into her own recesses of life and find a smile for herself, so that she can feel the happiness I felt in the presence of her and her Kunama brothers and sisters...the refugees currently living in UNHCR's Shimelba camp along the border of Ethiopia and Eritrea in a place not marked on a map.

(written 4 September 2005)

A Walk Through Africa's Largest Open-Air Market

Reputed to be the largest open-air market in Africa, Addis' Merkato is many blocks wide and stretches several blocks long in the heart of the city's Muslim community. Their main mosque is located within Merkato.

One can find whatever s/he may need in the market. We set out looking for a very specific umbrella: the rainbow colored one used by the parking ticket women. No, they do not hand out fines. They put little tickets under your windshield wiper marking the time you pulled up and parked your car. When it is raining, you can easily spot them by the rainbow-colored-pie-chart-looking bumbershoots held over their heads. My wife thinks the umbrellas are pretty. I find them practical, as they are quite large. Last Saturday, we went to Merkato in hopes of finding our prize along the way.

We set out first for the spice section, passing by the herbs and incense section first. Women with deeply-wrinkled skin sat by their offerings spread out before them on cloth. I recognized the cinnamon and cloves, but the other bark-like items had me baffled. Language barriers prevented me from learning the names and uses. None to worry, I was quite happy to be in the setting: exotic food stuffs, elbow-to-elbow people, warm sunny sky, and those imprint-on-the-brain images you enter markets for in the first place.

She was sitting behind her herbs and a few grains. Skin brown as mud and a few teeth in her chuckle. Gray hair wisping out from her dark blue head scarf. Thin well-used arms and long fingers pointing towards me. And over her eyes, black framed glasses with perfect round lenses thick like magnifying glasses. I immediately thought her to be a woman of profound knowledge of concoctions. How I wanted to be her pupil, a fleeting thought interrupted by her neighboring marketer trying to sell me an incense burner.

We soon found the curries and pepper spices of yellows, golds, mustards, burnt reds, rusts and flame oranges that sat in sacks tended by smiling women. Me being the curious one, I had to taste them. They obliged the strange white guy, handing me scoops to dab a finger at. I did. Laughs went around as I made some faces and gestured some smiles of my own. Only one pepper spice lingered on my tongue longer than I would have liked.

Across the street we stepped into the veggies and chickens stalls. Potatoes, onions, tomatoes, leeks, peppers and cabbage were seen in every direction. The chickens were squished into cages made from tree branches bent to make a dome cage that stood rooster-head high. The cobbles beneath our feet were wet and muddy from an early morning rain. The smell was one of sewage.

Onward and upward, we came to the traditional clothing area. Stall after stall of beautiful traditional Ethiopian dresses and shirts was the highlight of our time in the market. We twisted and turned through narrow passageways admiring handcrafted clothing of a fine quality similar to white linen hanging above and beside us. To our surprise, we noticed that nearly all of the seamstresses were men. We later thought that maybe the seamstresses were mostly men because it is men that have the money to buy the sewing machines. Who knows? Nevertheless, the talent on display in their tiny "stores" was second to none. Patterns and designs of all colors, and rooted in Ethiopian Christian Orthodox Church images, were threaded by hand. The men were warm and very polite, giving us several "welcome to my country" greetings as we walked through their obviously proud artwork. We told them we would return to buy a few pieces another day.

The quiet pathways of the clothing area gave way to the horns and choking diesel fumes of the street. We crossed over and circled around to an old bank that was converted to an indoor selling area. We made way to a small restaurant on the third floor for a rest of feet and to have a drink. Orange Fantas were sipped as we talked about things I no longer remember.

Still without the umbrella, we decided to begin walking in the direction of our home to exit Merkato and find a taxi. Whether we found the umbrella or not mattered less to us. We were getting hungry. Lunch was weighing more heavily on our minds. Besides we could come back with our Ethiopian friends and get one in a few minutes time.

Not out of the market yet, we walked by stands selling more belts than I thought could ever be found in one spot. Belts and men's underwear were everywhere.

And then a man carrying foam mattresses piled 10 high on his head. At 8 or so inches a pad, carrying the stack was a feat made more difficult by his having to dodge cars and car-dodging people.

And the bucket man. He carried a stack of purple buckets length wise over his shoulder. The stack was around 20 feet long, 10 feet of Barney dinosaur purple plastic going out in both directions from the shoulder. Somehow he managed to not knock anyone on the head in the twenty seconds I walked behind him.

Before we knew it, we were on the edge of Merkato. We decided to keep walking, having given up on the umbrella. We soon flagged down a taxi and scored our first honest price for a ride. We headed off for an Italian restaurant at Amist Kilo, a traffic circle on the main road heading north through the city, for some grub.

Later, umbrella-less and full-stomached, we departed for home. We experienced Africa's largest market unscathed, meaning no pickpockets, the only negative claim-to-fame of Merkato. I left the market wanting to go back.

****

There is something about being in a market that fills me. There is a pulse there, an energy that gets at the very essence of life. The buying of goods for life's survival. Basics for daily needs. A true free market economy at my fingertips, where my senses are heightened.

Watching fellow human beings going about their lives…where are you taking those purple buckets? How many chickens did you sell today? How long did it take you to sew that dress? How did you come to sell spices and not belts? Why did you buy that incense and not the other?

(written 11 September 2005)

Happy Ethiopian
New Year—1998

So you think it is 2005? Getting ready to celebrate 2006 in a couple of months? Hold on! It is only 1998 here in the ancient land of Ethiopia .

What?

The centuries-old Ethiopian calendar marks the birth of Christ as being 1000, 900, and 98 years ago and not 2000 and 5 years ago. The New Year holiday is celebrated every year on September 11th and not January 1st.

****

While many in the world were remembering New York and focusing attention on New Orleans , Ethiopians were slaughtering thousands of sheep and goats in their backyards and roasting them over open fires, the New Year's traditional meal for everyone regardless of ethnicity or religious conviction. Smoke rose from homes across Addis creating a lazy haze that hung like a New Year's hangover throughout the day.

****

The Addis Sheraton Hotel set off fireworks on New Year's Eve that woke me from my sleep. I went to the window to see if I could see the Chinese inventions exploding in the night sky, but to no avail. I lie back down only to be shocked from my slumber by the loudest booms I have ever heard. More than three miles away, the Sheraton set off explosions that rattled the windows in our home. I imagined that the adrenaline that coursed my through my veins from my initial fear maybe was not too unlike the adrenaline coursing the veins of the people living in today's war zones. I then recanted my thoughts, considering them unfair to war's victim witnesses. More explosions were set off at the Sheraton. I could not find another way to describe them. They were bomb-like. I am certain that if I was down at the hotel, my organs would have rattled inside my body while standing there.

****

Stuck between two calendars, 1998 and 2005, being in Ethiopia puts me in a predicament that has me question: When is the millennium change? What was Y2K? When was I born and how old am I? When was Jesus born? What has my education taught me? Does any of this matter when I live in a world where rhythms seem beyond "ancient" and "time-ness?" Are calendars humanity's attempts to lasso control of the "whys" we cannot answer?

****

It rained all day in Addis on New Year's Day. We stayed home and watched some of the festivities going on throughout the country via Ethiopian TV, the only channel broadcasted in the country. We watched traditional dancing, fascinated by the shoulder and head movements that reminded us of "popping," breakdancing style. My wife laughed as I tried to copycat what I saw on the TV.

****

Some people's lives are a day of sadness, sorrow and loss on September 11th. Others may get angry, understandably so. Here there is happiness and joy on the same day. Families reunite, eat, drink, sing, dance, laugh and do all the things that we do to celebrate the change of year.

Two calendars that have come into my existence have the same day, but have different meanings. Yet, because of the current world order, Ethiopians know of the Gregorian calendar's 9-11 significance, while the reverse cannot be said.

Today I am both 31 and 24 years old. I think I'll celebrate my youth.

(18 September 2005)

We are a Bouncing Kaleidoscope Playground Ball

Children walk home from school in the early evening light that artistic photographers dream of. Everything has taken on a fresh coat of sun-splashed colors: reds and yellows, especially, burst into the retina, but are tempered by the warm glow of many shades of beautiful brown skin radiating a wholesomeness emanated in the smiles and laughter shared by classmates and friends.

Kenny Rogers' "Evening Star" flows out of the car speakers like a soothing mountain creek. A dry blue sky with puffy white clouds that haven't spilled rain in two days is welcomed by the people of Addis. I find solace in the man chopping wood by the roadside, not too unlike the people back home who chop wood to feed the bellies of their woodstoves in winter. Another man, 50-something years old I would guess and dressed in a suit that he has probably had longer than I have been out of school, rides a beach cruiser bike, probably on his way home after a day at the office.

Many folks carry plastic grocery bags filled with the soon-to-be supper that they bought at the local roadside stands, butcheries, and grocers. The commonness between these food gatherers and the south central Pennsylvania food gatherers stopping at farmers' roadside stands, Myer's, Nell's or Weis Markets on the way home from work resonates in that place somewhere inside of me where reason and logic are not able to shed a light on.

In that moment of peace, when I cast away the questions of why things are the way they are, allowing my eyes to see life on its surface and without need to dig and bring to the surface its ugliness, I float above my own existence, taking refuge in the arms of present-tense. The schoolboy smiling and waving as we pass by is simply what he is, a schoolboy with an authentic smile as big as the Ethiopian sky sprawled out over our heads. He motions his right hand back and forth to say "Hello." The image locks itself in my heart, and I am in love with humanity.

The humanity to which I am bound up in, rolling along like a kaleidoscope playground ball bigger than a teacher's globe, is no longer me and you and them. I am the kaleidoscope playground ball called WE bouncing all around, up and down, in a being that cannot be defined because it is always changing. You are WE. They and them are WE. Together WE are going in the direction of nowhere, content in the state of US, the palm-side of WE, thriving in the non-need. WE are US.

WE are US standing by the roadside waiting for the bus to carry us back to our loved ones, having a cup of tea or coffee with our friends at Bilo's Pastry on Debre Zeit Road, walking hand-in-hand with our little ones as WE cross the street, and cooking ears of corn on mini charcoal stoves...

...the silhouetted lines of banana tree leaves flutter in the late evening breeze. Fluttering like "Flutterby", the butterfly that lights on a little girl's shoulders and brings into our world the raw emotions of wonder and discovery. Sitting on shoulders, its wings pulsating slightly up and down, the breath of life fills the girl's lungs and dances its way through her blood, journeying all the way from her tippy toes to the roots of her braided hair.

Night is not too far off, and Kenny's "Evening Star" wished for earlier is now twinkling above a neighbor's bean-pole-straight twin eucalyptus trees. The smell of roasting coffee wafts on the calm light air. I hear the sound of a pestle, gripped by another neighbor's experienced female hands, pounding peppers into the mortar to make berbere, a spicy condiment that accompanies meals.

Tonight, I will lay down in the bed of solitude, the mattress of WE and the pillow of US providing comfort. My wife will be by my side, the tangible "in love" I am most grateful for. Wrapped up in our love, WE celebrate US, the kaleidoscope playground ball bouncing all around, up and down only to be picked up and tossed back and forth by the children with beautiful brown skin walking home in the artistic photographers' dream light.

(written 26 September 2005)

Meskel: The Finding of the True Cross

The 26th of September is the eve of Meskel, the "Finding of the True Cross," the day Orthodox Christian Ethiopians believe Jesus' cross was found many centuries ago. All over the country, bonfires called "Demera" were burned this past Monday evening to celebrate the coming day.

On the twenty-sixth, we headed for Meskel Square in the center of Addis Ababa for the one-of-a-kind event. Walking on Bole Road toward the main attraction, I felt for the first time what it might be like to be on a pilgrimage. Surrounded by believers while walking, my wife and I ducked into the shade whenever possible, taking refuge from the hot sun with some of the others on their way to Meskel.

Soon we were in our seats on the terraced grass amphitheater only a few rows back from the front to the far right of the Demera. A sun-drenched sky pockmarked with a few cottontail clouds shined down on the biggest soon-to-be bonfire I have ever seen. From my vantage, the structure looked to be thirty feet high.

Bishops, priests, deacons, women and children dressed in colorful, and some magnificent, robes gathered around the Demera. Some groups paraded past us, singing songs, drumming large drums, chanting. Flags wishing peace and prosperity for Africa, the end of HIV/AIDS and other hopes unfurled as each group representing the many parishes of Addis shared their Meskel hopes with the crowd of on-lookers in the tens of thousands.

The excitement grew as 5:30 p.m. neared. The flatbed truck carrying the Lalibela and Aksum worshippers, complete with a band, worked the crowd into a frenzy. Singing traditional songs in Amharic, people rose to their feet and danced along. High-pitched ululating rang out from the revelers. I joined in with a little ululating myself.

The energy was high, the mood was festive. Goosebumps ran down my arms. I was as excited as those around me.

A few dignitaries played the political game before the lighting of the Demera. Speeches promising wealth and good health bored the people. Not soon enough, the rhetoric ended and the patriarch got up from his seat.

The people roared their approval. Deafening collective voices reminded me of the sound when the home team scores a touchdown.

A pep rally for Christ. Not in the evangelical, born-again way. I was at a spirited gathering of humanity that believed in the victory of their Jesus' cross.

The torches were lit. Flames danced off of them. The rising tide of anticipation and excitement grew ever louder. Gas was dumped on the wood and grasses making up the Demera.

"Burn it, Burn it," I said to my wife in a primal voice. Something about fire…

And then the ceremonial lighting of the bonfire occurred. Holy men and women quickly moved back from the huge flaming structure. The people cheered, sang and chanted. More ululating. More goosebumps.

The sun was setting as the Demera became fully engulfed in flames. Meskel was here. Meskel was alive.

×*****

This is the place to be right now. This is a celebration like no other. This is a mass of people singing in unison. This is dancing without looking over shoulders. This is a booming drum that reverberates in the soul. This is an ululation that pierces the heart and spills the blood of people who are willing to die on that cross. This is the Ethiopian Orthodox Church, the only African church that was a member, and still is, of the first gathering of the World Council of Churches. This is Ethiopia , the land where Christianity was first rooted on the African continent. This is Meskel. This is the Demera. This is where Ethiopia shines like the burning sun above.

****

Walking out to find a taxi to carry us home, we ran into two Ethiopian Good Shepherd Sisters we have befriended as part of our project. They are Catholic sisters. As they told us, all Christians can enjoy Meskel. They even added that everyone could come and enjoy Meskel. It is for everyone.

As one of the parish groups marched by us singing and drumming, I couldn't have agreed more. I believed that Jesus' cross was found, and that Ethiopia owned the right to have it...

...wherever it is.

(written 2 October 2005)

Put Fear and Danger Aside...
Write Your Own Story

The sun is shining these days. Like going to the sink and turning off the spigot, the rainy season came to an abrupt end. Suddenly, the Africa of my childhood visions, the story books, the classroom, the television has come into existence. Hot and sunny is the image of Africa, but my first two months in Addis was anything but that. No one talked of the rainy season at 7000 feet. It was cold.

This new-found knowledge leads me down the road of inquiry. Often, it is not until you have first-hand experience that you can say you have really learned anything. I think this is the case when learning about people and places. We can read the newspapers, watch the evening news, read the latest books and read the magazine articles. But, what are we really learning? How many of the story writers actually are on the ground when writing the stories?

How many of them are writing about the African bush from the comforts of modern hotels in capital cities? How many of the stories being told are from an African's view point? How much of the dangers and travesties of living and traveling in Africa are told by people that have experienced these dangers and travesties? How many of those stories come third and fourth hand?

I write these questions with only three months of living in Ethiopia. As you read this I am visiting the holy Islamic town of Harar in eastern Ethiopia. I will be on my way this afternoon to the town of Jijiga near the border with Somalia. Tomorrow I will visit a UNHCR camp for Somali refugees. This is an area that many would call off limits to travel. My wife and I have thoroughly researched traveling to the region. We have reports from partners who are working on the ground in Jijiga. They tell us that it is safe, that we will be fine. But if you were to ask local Ethiopians in Addis, they would warn you against traveling to the area. Part of it is legitimate concern, but for them, unfortunately, it has a little bit to do with racism as well.

Still, we will be mindful of where we are. I can only hope that this column does not prove to be hubris.

Many of you back home seem very concerned about our safety. While we completely understand where you are coming from and are most appreciative of your thoughts and prayers (and want them to continue!), we would like for you to know that we are doing well here. We are healthy. We are living amongst a people that are most respectful of us and are far more peaceful than some of your neighbors.

I am taking this space to address this notion of fear and perceived danger on the part of people of the West towards Africa. I am certain that if you were to come with a mind as wide open as the Ethiopian countryside, you would quickly find that there is little to fear and so much to look forward to. Pre-arrival dangers would be seen as worrying too much and soon give way to smiles and laughter. This is a beautiful land with inhabitants that want people to come and see their home, a home they are most proud of, as they should be. They are welcoming and always offer a warm sincere greeting. They will go out of their way to show their respect for you, to the point that you will feel uncomfortable with the attention given to you.

While I am no expert on Africa, I can tell you that Addis Ababa (and Ethiopia for that matter) provides little for any traveler to be afraid of. It is a place of endless discoveries, most of which will take place not in front of you, but inside of you.

It is the internal journey that really leads the travel-addicted to walk out their front doors. Landscapes and faces teach more than any book or news magazine could ever do. There is a quest for truth through experiential first-hand learning.

If you are going to learn of the African sun, you are going to have to stand under it. If you are going to learn about Ethiopia's rich history, you are going to have to go walk through its rock-hewn churches in Lalibela. If you are going to learn about cold-weather Africa, you are going to have to trek in the Simien Mountains in northern Ethiopia or live in Addis during the rainy season.

Lucky for you, and lucky for me, we can do this in relatively little danger or fear. And when we do, we will be able to write our own stories, stories that will allow us to differentiate between the realities and the non-realities being crafted in the newsrooms and classrooms across America.

(written 9 October 2005)

Heartfelt Joys
in Eastern Ethiopia—
A Traveler's Fortune

Meet Abdi. Abdi is from Harar in eastern Ethiopia . Abdi lives in Minneapolis with his wife and four children. Abdi is from Harar but lives in Minnesota? Let me explain.

My wife and I were in line for a complimentary sandwich and drink at Ethiopian Airlines' café because our late afternoon flight to Dire Dawa was delayed 45 minutes. Abdi was behind us in line. He asked us where we were from.

"The U.S. "

"Me too!!"

"Oh yeah...where from?"

" Minneapolis ."

****

Abdi left Ethiopia 24 years ago. He hadn't been back before this trip. He spent his first eight years living in Somalia before being sponsored by a Lutheran Social Services in Jacksonville, FL, where he lived for another eight years. He spent a few months in Denver after Florida, eventually settling in Minneapolis .

Why Minnesota? Abdi met his wife there. She too is from the Harar area. They are both of the Oromo people, and speak Oromo in their home in addition to English. Their four children speak Oromo, and dance the traditional dances of their parents' native land at weddings and other celebrations.

Abdi explained that a large Ethiopian/Somali community thrives in Minneapolis.

****

I am not sharing Abdi with you only to show that the American Dream is alive and well. I am sharing this story of Abdi with you because of what Abdi did for my wife and me. From the moment he met us, he displayed nothing but kindness and genuine friendliness. I wish I could say the same of my reactions to him. I was a little suspicious of him. Why was he so outgoing with us? Why was he so interested in us?

Our flight soon boarded and we were on our way. Passing by Abdi to take our seats, he told us he would negotiate a taxi to the bus station when we landed so that we would not get ripped off. He was going to Harar as well.

When the plane landed he took us under his wing the way a bigger brother would do for his younger siblings. The taxis were waiting outside the little airport office. He worked a price we could never get with our white skin in Ethiopia. (Hey, the reality is that traveling white folks in Africa have more money than most of the locals.)

The taxi carried us to the minibus. We were quickly packed into the minibus, twenty people in a bus that should hold maybe twelve at most. The windows were jammed shut. Abdi sat in the seat in front of us. Dire

Dawa to Harar is an hour's ride, at least. The entire way, Abdi asked if we were okay.

"Are you comfortable?" "How are you doing?" "I told the guy we will pay when we get out. Don't worry about getting your money out right now."

Hot, sweaty, and wanting nothing but to get out of that bus, we arrived in Harar in the dark, around 7:30 in the evening.

Harar is a mostly Muslim town. It is Ramadan, a time of fasting. No practicing follower of Islam eats between sunup and sundown. When the sun is down, the people eat great meals. The streets were filled with women selling fatiras—a fried dough pastry treat—and other food delights of Ramadan. Crowds of people were on the streets, walking around town and visiting each other's homes.

We got out of the minibus and Abdi told us that he was going to walk us to our hotel. Another man decided to walk with us because he knew exactly how to get to it. In a short five minutes or so, we were at the hotel. The other man wished us well and went on his way. Abdi stayed with us.

He met the hotel management, had them show us and him the room. Upon entering the room, he checked the lock to make sure that it was secure, not damaged. He made sure the price was fair. When all was settled, he asked if we were satisfied. We said yes. We thanked him for accompanying us throughout our trip. He said "you're welcome."

Humility. As he walked out of the room he said, "Maybe we'll meet again. In Minnesota or Pennsylvania."

****

When you travel in lands where language and culture is not familiar, there are times when you find yourself putting complete trust in a stranger. We are taught from a very young age to not talk to strangers. While this is probably a good parenting strategy, it does make for not being suspicious of fellow human beings very difficult in later life.

Abdi made our travel from Addis to Harar much smoother than it would have been without him. Sure, we would have managed, but it would have been more of a hassle, especially getting the taxi, bus and hotel room.

I wonder if Abdi was our guardian angel. At the same time, I do not like to think that he was something beyond our common existence. Rather, I believe Abdi is what we humans can be.

I hope that wherever his head lies down tonight, that it does so in peace.

Let us offer a collective wish of peace for Abdi and his family as they live out their American Dream.

(16 October 2005)

Heartfelt Joys in Eastern Ethiopia—Harar's Charm

We woke to no water in the hotel and a bright blue sky. The legendary town of Harar was outside, waiting for us to explore its more than 350 walkways, paths, and alleys that sit inside the predominately Muslim-occupied walls.

Harar is two towns in one: the renowned walled old city and the outlying mostly Christianized neighborhoods. People travel to Harar to see old Harar with its centuries-old homes and shops, and its Hadari people dressed in colorful garb. For Muslims and non-Muslims alike, Harar's 87 mosques found inside the four mile circumference of the 40 feet high, 800 year-old stone walls are equally fascinating.

The water came on. We showered. Girma offered to be our guide for a fair price. The watch showed 10:37 in the morning.

We entered the city through Shoa Gate, marked in Arabic script above its entrance. Immediately we were in the midst of village life.

Women carrying wood on their heads. Chickens scratching at the cobblestones. Vegetables and fruit being sold by squatting women. Old world lives, if I can call it that, existed in a modern context. A few satellite dishes could be seen on rooftops.

Walking on, we were satisfied in people-watching and snapping photographs. Around every corner more pathways seemed to go out in every direction. The walkways were never straight, always bending, twisting and meandering. We never knew what was waiting around the next turn.

****

Girma shared historical facts along the way:

Harar's gates were closed at night back in the day. If you were not inside by the time the gates closed, you slept outside.

The gates and walls were built by Muslims to keep Christians and the local, native Oromo people out. They were built for protection.

The British explorer Robert Burton was the first European to visit the town. The year was 1854.

The boy-wonder French poet Arthur Rimbaud came to Harar in 1880 and settled in and remained as a trader and photographer after abandoning poetry at age 19.

Ethiopia's last Emperor, Haile Selassie, grew up in Harar.

Today, Muslims and Christians get along fine in Harar. Some Christians do live inside the walls, and there is one church inside the walls.

****

"It looks like southern Spain," my wife said, referring to the whitewashed and pleasing pastel blues painted on the exterior walls of some homes along the pathways.

"Kind of looks like pictures I've seen of Greece," I added.

"Jerusalem too. I imagine Jerusalem looks a little like this," she responded.

Harar sits along an historical trade route that saw Egyptians, Middle Easterners, and Indians travel in from the Red Sea, the Gulf of Aden and the Indian Ocean. Spices, teas, and grains were exchanged through bronze, coffee and yellow-brown hands.

The Muslim market was a flurry of activity in the late-morning hours. Hawkers were selling their wares, all the while looking at us as we stopped to pose for a photograph by beautiful multi-colored baskets lying on the ground basking in the sun. Hadari women balanced jugs of water on their heads, a feat I will never be able to do.

Donkeys carrying wood for cooking trotted past, guided by girls and women on their way home or to the market to sell the wood. Our project works to alleviate the unhealthful impacts of smoke in the home attributed to cooking. The leading cause of death in children under the age of five in the developing world, according to the World Health Organization, is: complications resulting from poor indoor air quality. How many children of Harar will die prematurely because of the wood being carried in rawhide satchels on the sides of the donkeys?

Some would call it "cultural," this way of cooking. Romanticizing a wood-fired cooking stove, the idea that stoking the fire to feed a family is okay for the world's poor, is all too often offered by perpetrators of the "cultural" arguments. That these "culturalists" can stand at the gas or electric stove in their homes preparing a meal and contend with the politically and academically-accepted "cultural" position, in some political and academic circles, angers me.

****

Our day ended with a meal atop a hotel that looks over the Christian market situated along the hard road outside of the Shoa Gate. Most interesting were the chat sellers. Chat is a bushy plant with leaves that are mildly intoxicating. Chat-chewing is a part of life here not too unlike going out for beers with friends. While it is mostly men that chew chat, women are known to chew as well.

A chat ceremony consists of friends sitting around on a blanket with bags of chat and sodas within arms-reach. You pull the leaves off the stems and stuff them into your cheek like tobacco. The drinks are for putting flavor into your mouth. The ceremony can last for hours. Its effects are first noticed by people becoming talkative and animated, kind of like caffeine. Life apparently becomes more easy-going and happiness falls upon you.

No, I didn't chew any chat. Not because I thought it was a drug. It seemed to me that chat-chewing was an innocent activity no different than spending an afternoon at the coffee shop. Later, however, I would learn that it can be a social illness among men.

For me, I did not like the idea of chewing on green leaves that maybe could have carried a microbe that would have had me bed-ridden for a day or two. I did not want to take a chance at ruining a perfect day exploring one of the last great, and little-traveled, destinations on planet Earth.

(written 23 October 2005)

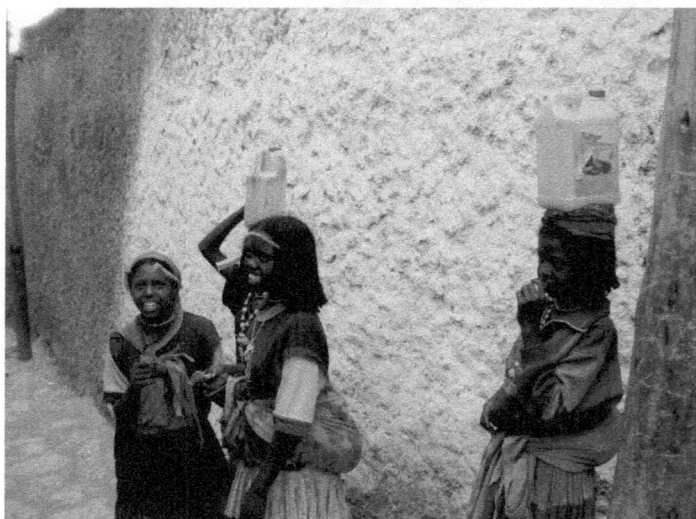

Heartfelt Joys in Eastern Ethiopia—Kebrebeyah Refugee Camp

The UNHCR Kebrebeyah refugee camp occupies a vast plain of land on the edge of a harsh desert that marches to the southeast where it takes on the name Ogaden. Only thirty-five miles from the Somalia border, some of the Somali people have been living in the camp since the beginning of the civil war that broke out in their homeland fifteen years ago. We were visiting the camp to assess the Somali people's satisfaction and use of our project's 130 stoves that we placed there a few weeks before.

****

"Thank Allah for the people who brought us this stove. Thank Allah for the stove. Thank Allah for this project. Allah, bless these good people."

More than one woman expressed thanks and gratitude to Allah for us and our work.

It is a somewhat surreal experience when a person thanks a god you do not know for your life and your work. I know very little about Islam. What I do know is that an offer of camel's milk, a very nutrient-rich drink that helps keep the Somali people relatively healthy, and a sentiment of "you are a good man" seem to speak to our shared human existence. I accepted her blessings. Allah's blessings.

****

My wife documented a woman's injuries that she sustained while gathering wood for cooking. She went out in the morning and returned eight hours later in the rain. She had a bundle of wood on her back. The weight of it and the slippery mud caused her to fall. She severely injured both her hands and arms, probably breaking the one wrist. While writing down her story, other women came forward and told their stories of gathering fuel wood.

Many talked of being beaten with sticks and fists by local men. The men stole their wood after the beating. Others talked of knowing women who have been raped while collecting wood, a well-documented, unfortunate reality for Africa's women. Though none of them admitted to being raped themselves, they talked of friends who have been raped. Is there any difference among the women of the world who have been violated yet struggle to tell their own story? It is always someone they know, never them. When will we give them the support they need to tell their stories? When will they stop having to tell such horrific stories?

Our project's mission took on greater importance after talking with the women. All the women wanted a stove. All of them talked of how they hated gathering wood. How it hurt their backs. How the girls missed school several days a week. Cooking with wood starts in the pre-dawn hours when women walk out from their homes to gather fuel.

I prayed to Allah that the women would find healing.

****

"Buy my baby. I don't want my children. I have 3 anyway. I need the money. Buy my baby." A desperate mother relays her desires to me through a Somali-to-English translation.

No matter how much you hear about this kind of thing occurring, no matter how many articles you read, you are never prepared for the look in a mother's eyes when she wants you to buy her child. It disturbs you in places you did not know existed. A darkness creeps over you and you realize that there are inequalities and injustices in life that will never be addressed in any policy or government debate.

Life can be an awful thing.

****

Somali homes look like large dome camping tents. They are constructed by women. A wood-stick frame is set up, and is then covered by plastic donated by the UN. They then pile old clothes and blankets over the plastic, giving them the look of a ragged quilt grandma made back on the farm.

I noticed an Oxford University sweatshirt adorning the outside of one of the homes. I thought of the irony of that sweatshirt, the prestigious university on display on the house of one of the world's poorest families. That sweatshirt's cost maybe equaled the family's yearly income.

****

Somalis welcomed us wherever we went, especially the children. I shook their hands, sharing a greeting of "Selam." I played marbles with them, they laughing at my inability to shoot the marble. We walked with airplane arms and high-stepped from house to house. I made weird noises with my mouth; they echoed my silliness.

They surrounded me as I sat under a shade tree. They felt the hair on my arms. They touched my white skin and stared at my hair. I lowered my head and let them touch it. They laughed. I laughed.

Allah, bless the children.

****

Somehow, amidst such depressing living conditions, we left the camp overjoyed. I have yet to place a finger on it, but there is something that makes time passed in such dire places a positive experience. I wish I knew why I was so happy when I left the camp. I was happy in my thoughts, and at the same time I was sad because I did not want to leave.

I offered them a prayer, "Allah, shine down goodness on the Somali people living in Kebrebeyah and all Somali people everywhere. Help them find a way to end their country's strife so that they can return to the place of their birth."

(written 30 October 2005)

Our Return to the Land of Enchantment

After spending a little over a month in Nigeria, we returned to Ethiopia. We had a lot of work waiting for us in Addis. In fact, as you are reading this, my wife and I will have just returned from four days in the Ogaden Desert, located in the far southeastern region of Ethiopia. Our project placed fifty stoves in the town of Denan, site of an Internally Displaced Peoples camp, meaning the people living there are not refugees because they are Ethiopian citizens. They are Somali, and have been forgotten about by the Ethiopian government and are little-known to the outside world. Without question, they are living in abject poverty.

Prior to our trip to the Ogaden, which was the first full week of December, we made a trip to the United Nations Shimelba refugee camp in the north. We visited the camp back in August. This recent trip was a follow-up to gather more data for a report we have to write that will hopefully convince the UN High Commissioner for Refugees (UNHCR) to include our project within its 2006 budget. If things work out, we may even be granted official Implementing Partner status with the UNHCR.

I am writing this column on December 1st, World AIDS Day. The climate outside is what I consider to be ideal living conditions. The afternoon is warm and sunny, temps in the high 70s. The sky is the cliché, robin's egg blue. Nights are cool, chilly, though my wife describes it as very cold. At 7500 feet above sea level, it does get cold overnight.

A few days ago my body was rocked by a gastrointestinal illness. After more than five months of eating in Africa, I had finally gotten sick. I suspect it was injera, a fermented flatbread that is eaten with every traditional meal in Ethiopia. You use it to eat your meal with your hands. Forks and spoons are not used when eating injera.

My stomach was racked with pain, and blew up like a balloon. Filled with gas that needed to exit, I even belched up rotten egg smelling burps. Soon the diarrhea came, and my night was sleepless. I popped some cipro into my mouth, and decided I was not going to eat anything in the morning so that the microbes would have nothing to feed on. Two more cipro pills and things settled down. By evening I was feeling better. I went to bed around eight o'clock and woke up the next morning a brand new man.

While we were away in Nigeria, opposition party protesters held rallies against the current Ethiopian administration. The rallies were a response to the May election results. Sadly, the government sent out the police and military to quell the protesters. The press reported that forty-one people were killed this time, though university student students say the number is probably around one-hundred. A hundred or more were also wounded. Add this to the June protests where thirty-two people were killed, and Ethiopia's political circumstance has now reverted to its bloody past.

Our guard here at the office, a peaceful man in his early fifties, named Tarafi and who my wife adores, worries about his son. More than two-thousand boys and men were picked up off the street during the recent rallies by the military and carried away to prison camps outside of Addis. His son was in the wrong place at the wrong time. He does not know when he will be released.

The opposition party was also arrested and placed in jail, their crime being that they engaged in activities that were unconstitutional. The future of democracy in Ethiopia is a bleak picture.

Despite this reality, a reality that is all too common in Africa, we are happy to be back in Ethiopia. It is nice to walk the streets amongst such gentle people. I have not concretely figured it out yet, which is fine with me, but there is something very special about this country and its people, even though it has endured several decades of war. I have often told people that I think Guatemala is a magical place (it too has a horrific history over the past couple of decades), something about the colors and the Maya.

Ethiopia is like that, but maybe the correct way to describe it is as an enchanting place.

I like that. Ethiopia—the Land of Enchantment.

(written 18 December 2005)

Shimelba Refugee Camp

In the far north of Ethiopia, along the border with Eritrea, sits the Shimelba refugee camp. The camp is occupied by primarily Tigray and Kunama peoples, with a few other ethnic groups, notably the Saho, filling out the population. The majority of the refugees are men, most of them having fled military conscription in their native country, a former state of Ethiopia prior to the civil war that ended in 1991 with the fall of the Dergue, a communist regime with its stronghold in faraway Addis at the time.

We returned to the camp to check up on our stove project. Having been there in late August, early December gave the people an additional four months to become familiar with the ethanol-fueled stove. This time around the landscape was not the rainy season-fed greens that led us to believe that the region was able to easily grow food.

The land was every shade of khaki for as far as we could see. We saw the rocky soil that was hidden under the teff, a nutrient rich grain native to the highlands of Ethiopia, back in August. Families were in the fields harvesting the year's teff, scythes in hand and legs folded under them as they slowly did their work.

If the rains do not come next year, will the people survive?

****×****

"I used to dream. I no longer am able to dream. I don't know if I will ever get out of here. I used to be an engineer. I used to have my own business…I had a future.

I escaped by hiding in a church after a friend's wedding in a town near the border. We stayed there until the sun went down. We would move only at night. When the sun came up, we would hide out in homes along the way. Then at night, we would walk for another 6-7 hours. When we finally made it to the border, the Ethiopian military were actually nice to us. They told us where to get the bus and how to get to the camp. I guess for them it is fewer enemies to fight if this war breaks out again." -Samson

****

The Shimelba refugee camp is like few other camps around the world. A good portion of the Tigrigna refugees are from the Eritrean capital of Asmara. Educated, urban, and having some money, they set up what amounts to a small town in the camp. Using the money they were able to carry with them, they set up pool halls, cafes, and more than one digital satellite TV, accounting for the comforts of their former lives. No electricity running to the camp, lighting is powered by generators.

Such a scene can lend itself to presenting a different understanding of a refugee camp. Dirt and squalor are what we imagine a refugee camp to be. It is that too, as is evidenced by walking across the camp to where the Kunama people live.

But while listening to Don Williams croon out from a stereo at a local café, I got to thinking about our notions of refugees and how they live. Moreover, I had to ask myself why I thought that the amenities of an Asmaran lifestyle did not seem to fit the place I was occupying.

Why can't African refugees have a TV to look at while drinking a Coke with a pool stick in hand? Does this make them less of a refugee? Why do we accept the image of a sub-Saharan African refugee as one who has dirty, torn clothes and little to eat? Do we need children to have flies crawling in and out of their mouths (I did see this on the Kunama side) for them to be a refugee?

A refugee is stuck. S/He tries to make the best of their life. If the best does not adhere to my definitions of what their "best" should be, then shame on me. Shame on me for my luxurious world view and shame on me for being able to come and go as I please.

(written 15 January 2006)

An Afternoon in Axum , Great African Empire 2000 Years Ago

Axum is a dusty little town in the north of Ethiopia , one of four stops along the country's historic route, a route that is steeped in rich Orthodox Christian traditions in a land that was legendary to the Romans and the peoples of the Middle East . Today, Axum is still a place of legends.

Stone obelisks weighing several tons reaching anywhere from 10 to 60 feet into the majestic blue sky stood like ancient monks before us. The tallest of them all, nearly 100 feet long, lay broken in three parts on the grass. The most ornate one sat cut up in three shipping crates; the Italian government decided to return it to Ethiopia where it rightfully belonged. The main field is no bigger than half a football field, but the presence it bestowed upon us was larger than life. How did they get them to stand up? How did they carve them?

It is believed that when masons were done chipping away at the patterns and designs, the obelisks were pulled into position by elephants. Once in the hole that served as the base, hundreds of men pulled the stones into place. But why did they construct them?

Tombstones. The obelisks are huge grave markers befitting of the men below, kings.

Axum is considered by some scholars to be one of the greatest empires of recorded history, up there with the Egyptians, Romans, and Persians. The kingdom of Axum controlled areas that today reach into Egypt, Saudi Arabia and the Holy Land . The Axumites traded along the Red Sea and into the Indian Ocean.

Walking up a hill on our way to see the remains of King Kaleb's Palace, we paused briefly to see the Queen of Sheba's Bath. Now a small reservoir where local women and girls wash their clothes and collect buckets of water for cooking, it was at one time the place where the fabled Queen cleaned up. Our guide pointed to the steps cut into the rock, "That is where the Queen of Sheba entered the pool."

Surrounded by sheep, cattle, and the men and boy shepherds who guided the animals, I thought of home and how the rural scene before me was familiar despite the brown hillsides and African farmers around me. Kicking up dust as they went, the boys looked hardened by life, only twelve years into it.

We stopped at a small shack to the left of the road. Inside was a rock with scripture scribed on it, but it was not just any ole scribe. It was written in Ge'ez, the ancient language of Ethiopia, Greek, and Hebrew. The connection between the highlands of Ethiopia and the outside world could be seen there on that rock sitting inside a little wooden house.

Twenty minutes later we were down inside King Kaleb's tomb. Dark, home to bats, and quiet, we shined a headlamp on the walls. Tightly fitted together with pinpoint precision, literally, my wife was reminded of the old Inca walls of Cuzco, Peru . Big blocks of granite fit together like puzzle pieces, and yet few people have ever heard of the Axumites. An African Empire, Great Civilization of History, and we read nothing about it in our history books.

On the way back down the hill into town, we could see the top of St. Mary of Zion church shining in the bright afternoon sun. Inside the modern exterior walls are seven chapels built on top of one another. It is believed that inside the seventh chapel is the Ark of the Covenant. All Ethiopian Orthodox believers know that the tablets held in Moses' hands on Mt. Sinai are inside St. Mary of Zion church. The priest that watches over the chapel says he has gone as far as the sixth chapel. If he were to set his eyes on the Ark, he would go blind.

Would it not be worth going blind if you could see the Ten Commandments? We could all walk blindly into God's Kingdom. Don't we do that now anyway?

Tired and thirsty, we walked back into the center of town and found a little café for a rest. Sharing out thoughts of the day and what we had learned, my wife and I wondered about how much of what we had been taught over the years was true. What do our history books not teach us? How accurate is our perception of history?

I don't know, really.

But I do know that saying "All Hail the Axumites, great people of Africa and the World" feels right!

****

The historic route of Ethiopia includes Axum, Lalibela, Gondar and Bahar Dar. My wife and I were able to visit Lalibela and Gondar as well. Over the next two weeks, we will continue on the journey, stopping next in the holy mountain village of Lalibela, site of what some consider to be the 8th Wonder of the World—Lalibela's 11 rock-hewn churches. The churches are mind-boggling in how they were constructed. After Lalibela, we will go to Gondar , home of 300 year old castles and a tiny church with an angelic ceiling.

And then we'll head out east and travel to the Ogaden Desert of Ethiopia, a remote region of the Earth where my wife and I had our souls touched by followers of Islam in a place called Denan. We will finish up where camels by the thousands come to quench their thirsts.

(written 22 January 2006)

Searching for Holiness in Lalibela's 11 Magnificent Rock-Hewn Churches

Sitting in what was a tomb dug into the side of the wall sat an elderly monk wrapped in a yellow robe. He was holding a tattered copy of scripture, rocking to and fro in deep meditation. Other priests and monks stood along the walls, some looking up at the impressive rock church before them.

Cut from the bedrock over 800 years ago by King Lalibela's followers, it stands testament to the heart and soul of the first Christian kingdom of Africa, and is the holy center of the Ethiopian Orthodox Church.

Mid-morning. The sun is already high in the clear blue mountain sky above the holy village. Perched on a hillside 8000 feet above the sea, deep in the mountains of Abyssinia, with an escarpment on the eastern side of town that reaches up to 12,000 feet, Lalibela is also home to Africa's mountain farmers, herders of sheep and goats, dressed in woolen robes. The site plays host to Western tourists decked out in the latest high-tech travel gear.

My wife and I set out with our guide to visit the eleven rock churches of Lalibela. Legend has it that King

Lalibela had the churches built to show God his devotion to Him, and that they were completed within a century. Masons worked from sunup to sundown. Then the magic began. Angels descended from heaven during the night to give a helping hand to the believers. The angels saw what was being done and knew God would be happy.

Listening to the meditations going on around us, the feel of warm sun on our faces, standing at the bottom of the church and looking up 70 feet to the church's roof, I knew that angels did indeed come down and build these churches. Could humans really have cut into the earth from ground level and carved out churches complete with windows and doorways with rudimentary tools? How did they do it so that each church is only one piece of rock?

More than anything else I have seen in my life-from the pyramids of the Aztecs and Mayas to the Golden Gate Bridge-Lalibela's churches were bigger than my mind. I could not grasp the magnitude of undertaking such an architectural feat. "They built down, not up," I said to myself. From ground level, you cannot see the churches until you are on top of them.

Impressive. Magnificent. Words fail to describe their greatness.

We toured the first cluster consisting of six churches, walking in and out of narrow passageways and tunnels to get from one to the other. A small room cut into the one passageway was home to the nuns, women who have devoted their lives to meditating on the teachings of Christ.

A little beyond the cluster along a dirt trail stood the church of St. George, the patron saint of Ethiopia. The most famous of the churches, its cross-shaped roof could be seen as we crested a small rise in the trail. Having seen it on Ethiopian tourism signs, postcards and books, I still was not prepared for its beauty. I stood in awe, feeling like maybe I was a pilgrim. How I wanted to believe in something at that moment.

But, I could not. Earlier in our walk we visited one of the churches that housed a replica of Jesus' tomb. My wife was not permitted to enter the room of the tomb. Her female-ness deemed her unworthy to enter.

I was angered by the priest's decree that women cannot enter the room.

Wasn't it women who prepared Jesus' body for his true tomb? Didn't Jesus appear to a woman, Mary Magdalene, first after his rise from death? Wasn't it from a woman that Jesus was born into our world?

We took a break for lunch before seeing the final cluster of 4 churches. They, too, did not disappoint in their architectural wonder. Once inside, we were transformed into a place of holiness, where scripture books, paintings and frescoes dated back to anywhere from 400-800 years. Gold, bronze, and silver crosses mounted on staffs were shown to us by the priests, each church having its own unique cross design. The one cross was said to have been brought to Lalibela from Jerusalem.

Our day in what some guidebooks consider to be more impressive than Jordan's Petra came to a quiet close. The late afternoon sun began to set over the rugged Simien mountain range. I thought of some people's notion that Lalibela should be granted "8th Wonder of the World" status. I could not think of the other seven. Why bother giving it such status?

A cup of hot tea was resting on my lips. My wife was sitting quietly beside me. How difficult it is to be a Christian woman. I wanted to feel that Lalibela was a place where I maybe could feel God's presence. A few times in the day I thought that I did, but they were erased by the denial of my wife's entry into the room. It was too fresh in my memory.

I know that Jesus would have allowed her to enter. He would have taken her by the hand and welcomed her into his church. He would have sat down with her, right there in one of Lalibela's rock-hewn churches, on the side of a mountain in Ethiopia, and shared his tomb with her. He would have shared a conversation with his equal, making Lalibela a living house of the holy.

(written 5 February 2006)

Gondar's Angel Eyes— A Pathway to Peace

Walking the mile and a half or so from our hotel to the Debre Berhan Selassie Church, the town of Gondar, our last stop along Ethiopia's historic route, was living out its typical Sunday afternoon routine. Families and friends talked in the street, men sat around drinking coffee at the cafes, and goats wandered about in the warm sun.

We were on our way to see the famous little church with its angelic ceiling. Soon enough we were paying the entrance fee and crossing the road to pass through the gate into the church yard. We quickly went up the entrance and removed our shoes. Stepping in, we looked up right away.

And there they were.

Heads of angels with beaming eyes covering the entire ceiling looked down upon us. Red and blue backgrounds with light brown faces filled with big, beautiful black onyx eyes and curly hair ran side to side, row after row from one end of the church to the other. My wife decided to lie down on the floor and look up. I followed her lead.

We could not help but wonder if this is what heaven may feel like, a place where angels watch over you.

74

Watching over us, the angels of Debre Berhan were the kind of comfort we all wished for when the bogey man was outside our windows at night when we were kids.

The walls, too, were covered in paintings. The crucifixion. The devil and hell. Many of the saints and scenes from the Bible stretched from corner to corner no bigger than fifty feet long and twenty feet wide.

Sitting on a bench along the one wall, we sat back and took it all in, observing the light coming in the top window. How wonderful it is to see other lands and paintings several centuries old.

The following morning we toured the Royal Enclosure, sometimes referred to as Africa's Camelot. Emperor Fasilades built the first castle inside the walls back in 1640, and emperors that followed him built subsequent smaller buildings, none coming close to the size and grandeur of Fasilades home. In the grand dining room and its adjacent dance hall, we easily imagined the big dinners and decadence that surely occurred centuries ago. My wife stole a dance from me, our bodies a silhouette against the large opened door.

We walked down the stone stairway, imagining the romances that may have occurred after dinner, us falling in love with the idea of love.

The falling in love dream ended quickly when a group of aging Italian tourists came onto the main lawn. Too much distraction. Up until then, we had the entire Enclosure to ourselves. Fortunately, we were finishing up our tour.

That night at a local restaurant we marveled at the crowd of a hundred or so spectators that gathered in the main dining area to watch the big soccer game on the satellite TV. It was a game out of England, and the people paid for a seat to watch the game much the way you would for a movie. Hooting, hollering and clapping reminded me of home and going to a bar in a sports town on a Sunday afternoon. Cheer on the team.

While leaving Gondar on the way to the airport, we talked to the taxi driver about the current political situation in the country. He was angry that the students were being killed and that men and boys were being rounded up by the thousands and sent off to prison for no reason.

Other than fear.

I thought of the fear in the politicians that leads them to do such things. And I thought of the fear in the men and boys on the backs of the trucks.

I wished that all of them, the accusers and the imprisoned, could lie down together on the floor and look up at those angel eyes on the ceiling of that little church in the mountains of their homeland. I thought that maybe, just maybe, they could see through those eyes a way forward that need not be violent and deadly.

I thought maybe all would see peace.

(written 5 February 2006)

A Place Called Gode

The airstrip at Gode was paved. This surprised me, considering that we were in the middle of nowhere in the Ogaden Desert, somewhere in far southeastern Ethiopia.

And that is exactly the lesson of nowhere versus somewhere. Paved airstrips should not be a measurement of where one is. Gode is somewhere, and for an hour or so and a night, it was my "here." But for thousands of people, Gode is home. "The middle of nowhere" is never an apt description of a location.

Sixty-four cases of medicines were accounted for. Dick, an independent filmmaker and man of genuine heart, was bringing yet another load of supplies for the tiny medical clinic that serves sixty-thousand living humans in Denan and its surrounding villages. Dick was in Denan in 2000 to document the famine that the outside world never heard of. Having visited and worked in over 100 countries, something about Denan stirred his soul. When the head elder expressed in plain words that maybe Dick could do something for Denan, Dick thought maybe so. Little did he know that five years later he would dedicate his life to a village on the edge of human consciousness.

We were with him to assess our stoves that were placed in the town. Our Director, Harry, met Dick on a flight back to the U.S. from Ethiopia. Dick thought Denan would be a good place for Project Gaia to extend its study; in the Ogaden, wood, the only cooking option, is scarce. Women and girls walk up to twelve hours and ten miles round-trip to gather fuel wood to feed their families.

The trucks were loaded with boxes of glucose bags, malaria treatment, bandages, and other healthcare needs of the clinic. We jumped in the back seat, anticipating the most adventurous two hour ride of our lives.

We stopped at a local cafe for lunch. Papayas were sat on the table. A knife was provided to cut them open. Our colleague, Muhktar, of the Ogaden Welfare and Development Association (OWDA), demonstrated the proper way to cut open the papayas for eating. Remembering my dislike of papaya despite the fact that I had a papaya tree in my backyard in Honduras, I declined his offer of a slice. At my wife's encouragement, however, I grabbed half of a papaya and sank my spoon into it. Ripened by forever sunshine, I enjoyed Gode's papaya.

Flame-grilled goat and Somaili-style spaghetti, spicy peppers and some onions minus the tomato sauce, were brought out to us on large plates. Hungry, and knowing we had to get on the road in order to make it to Denan before sundown, we chowed down quickly.

Satisfied, we set out north through town, our driver finding the right path through the neighborhoods. On the edge of town, we were stopped by the Ethiopian military checkpoint. Our paperwork was in order. We anticipated we would be given clearance within a few minutes, thus arriving to Denan well-before dark.

One and half hours later we were cleared to pass. The guard questioned Muhktar about our medical supplies. In the region, the Ogaden National Liberation Front (ONLF) has been raising an armed insurrection against the Ethiopian Government. We were suspected of carrying medicines to the ONLF. The glucose bags, much needed by wounded fighters, were the major glitch. Muhktar was patient with the military. We were too, waiting in the truck as dust blew and the sun beat down.

Permission to drive on was granted. Our driver hit the accelerator and we began our journey into the land of thorny bushes, dik-dik-the smallest specie of the antelope family-and thousands of camels.

(written 12 February 2006)

An Evening in Denan

The moon is rising over the thatched roof and mud-walled homes that sit idly in a cluster along the dirt road heading north out of Gode. Some forty miles or so from Gode, the cluster of homes is the town of Denan, a Muslim community of culturally Somali-Ethiopians living in one of the most inhospitable tracts of land on the planet.

Mats have been placed on the ground in the yard behind the house where we are staying. A tightly woven fence constructed from branches and twigs encloses the yard, the only deterrent to prevent the wild animals, mostly hyenas, from entering the family's living space.

We take a seat on the mats and rummage through our bags looking for the baby wipes we brought with us from Addis. We find them, soon wiping our faces, necks, and armpits. This serves as our shower for the day, and will for the next two days, as we are in a place where water is most limited, especially at this current time when the October rains never arrived a few months back. The onset of drought and its consequential famine can be seen in the inches of dust and dirt that is the soil.

A group of men have gathered on the opposite side of the yard. They stand shoulder to shoulder facing east. They recite prayers in unison. They bow and prostrate to Allah. Off in the distance, beyond the Ogaden, through anarchic Somalia, and over the Red Sea lies Mecca, the holiest of cities for these men. I watch them closely, thinking that I could be one of them, if only I had been born where they were born.

It takes a few baby wipes to feel clean. My wife is the only woman sitting amongst men in a world where men rule and women are ruled over and have little-to-no voice. She is so strong. The women of the house are hiding inside or over in the outside kitchen, occasionally passing by on their way between the two rooms, their colorful dresses blowing slightly in the night air.

Soon the local administrators arrive and we sit with them on the mats. Greetings are exchanged, our legs folded under us or crossed over so as to not have a foot pointing directly at the men. Doing so is considered an insult, a sign of disrespect.

Dick gives them an update on his efforts to bring water to the village. He speaks of the recent load of medical supplies he brought for the clinic. The administrators are pleased.

Our stove project has been well-received, they tell us. "But," they say, "We need more stoves." The people love the stove. They do not have to gather wood anymore. We explain that after the study is completed we may be able to bring more stoves. They seemed satisfied.

After they leave, we wait for the village elders to arrive, the true leaders of the community. Again, pleasantries are exchanged and we repeat what was said to the administrators. The elders add that it is okay for us to walk through the village the next day to assess the stoves in the homes. We are welcome to walk freely.

Hungry, the night is coming to a close. The moon is high above us, illuminating the yard enough to see everyone's faces. We talk with the local doctor about female genital mutilation, a serious concern in the region.

A large plate of plain spaghetti noodles is sat on the ground. We form a circle around it. Small tins of tuna are handed to each of us.

I grab my fork and dig in, adding the oily tuna to the noodles. My wife seems as "here-now" as she has been in a while. I am amazed at her courage; she was certain to share with the elders her concerns for the women of the village.

****

Tomorrow we will here from women of fourteen households that are using our stoves. They will tell us that they no longer go out to collect wood. The 10-12 hours of walking are over for them. They pray that we will bring more stoves to other women, that more ethanol will be available in the future.

(written 19 February 2006)

Gathering Water in Denan in a Time of Drought

Two little girls are gathering water on the far side of the oversized puddle-of-a-pond on the outskirts of Denan town. They are dipping their containers in the brown water. The one struggles to put the head-strap around her forehead, a bottle hanging down her back at the end of the rope. The other girl, her older sister, assists her. Then she puts her own head-strap on.

We watch as they walk towards us, the littlest one with one flip-flop on her right foot having a difficult time getting up the slight embankment. Again, her sister helps her out. Local boys watch us as we watch the girls.

"How old is she?"

"She is 3 years old," the response comes back through a Somali translation.

****

Right now, more than 11 million people are facing an extreme drought throughout southern and eastern Ethiopia , Kenya and Somalia. Battles have broken out in recent weeks over access to water holes. Cattle are dying. Children have resorted to drinking their own urine. Some have already perished in the relentless heat;

lives lost in what is looking like yet "another" African famine.

Aid agencies on the ground are sounding the sirens, hoping to awaken the big donors to step in with monies do that they can bring in food and water. They are saying it will likely be worse than the famine in 2000 in this part of the Horn of Africa.

What famine in 2000? Did we hear about it in the newspaper? On the evening news?

****

Soon we see cattle cresting the small rise behind the puddle-of-a-pond. They trample down the sand and into the water, gulping up water as soon as they enter. The girls turn towards home as the cattle enter one-by-one.

Do they cook with that water? Hopefully it comes to a boil. Hopefully they do not drink the water.

"Do you think they drink the water," drifts into the dry, Ogaden air, a depressing thought that none of us wants to answer. Too sad to think about.

****

Try to place your soul into the life of the girls. Where they are living right now is water-less. The photo was taken in early December. It has not rained one drop since then.

They have no water. NO WATER. From what I know, there is some water being trucked in. It is not enough. Temperatures are hitting above 100 degrees Fahrenheit.

I know, "What can I do about it?" Is that what you're thinking? If so, you're in luck. I have an answer.

The Denan Project. Remember Dick, the filmmaker I introduced you to a few columns back? He's the one who founded The Denan Project. I met him in Ethiopia and traveled to Denan with him. I assure you that he will see that each donation gets to the water project that he is working on in Denan. Simply earmark your donation as "Water Money." You have my word.

That's right, you can answer the question of "What can I do about it?" by going to your wallets and pocket books and getting out a dollar bill or two. Of course, 5s and 10s, or even 20s, would be better!!

Don't think about it, simply go do it. You give money to your government every day and it gets wasted. But, I guarantee that every cent you send will go to the people of Denan.

Ok, here's what you can do:

Donate online to The Denan Project, http://thedenanproject.com

****

Do you see it? The girls collecting water are happy. Instead of seeing them as dying of thirst, we see them drinking a refreshing, cool cup of water. THANKS TO YOUR BIG HEART and small donation THE PEOPLE OF DENAN WILL HAVE WATER.

(written 26 February 2006)

Shinile: 40 Wells and Thousands of Camels

From the roof of the beaten 1980s Land Cruiser, camels could be seen for as far as I could see across the vast stretch of open, desert-tan colored land. The sky overhead was blue like the way dry desert skies are at mid-day: impossibly blue. The sun was a shiny pale yellow disc hanging in that impossibly blue sky, and a soft breeze that sometimes got up the courage to be a gust of wind blew against me, across the humps of the camels, and over the daggers strapped behind the belts on the smalls of the back of nomadic Somali people.

Locals were eyeing us with curious caution. Some might have never laid their deep brown/black eyes on a white person. We were accompanied by an Ogaden native who spoke Somali, so the ice was broken through him; we were there to see a most fascinating place on earth.

Every day, bands of nomadic camel herders bring their camels to the forty salty wells of Shinile. Some may walk for days for this opportunity to fatten up their camels, the Somali lifeblood. Camels are used primarily for transportation and food. The nutrient-rich camel milk literally keeps the people alive, especially in times of little rain.

****

A dull ring emanates from the wooden bell hanging from a camel's neck. Each herder crafts his own bells, each bell having its own distinct sound which allows the herder to know where his camels are at all times.

Songs can be heard coming from the direction of one of the wells. Men are singing in unison as they pull up leather bags filled with water. Once brought up from the possibly one-hundred feet deep source below, the water is immediately dumped into a log trough where camel heads that were looking out at other camel heads quickly drop to the water-filled, hollowed-out log.

Too salty for human consumption but able to be processed by the camels, the wells maintain water year round in one of the driest places on the planet. Even more impressive, each well was hand-dug by the Somali herders.

****

"How long does each group get to drink?"

"About two hours."

"And the men pull up the water for two hours?"

"Yes. And they rotate around so you get a rest. But that's not always!"

"Is there a waiting line? How do you know which group goes next?"

"You must wait your turn. We know who came in when."

Stories of fights breaking out between groups are not uncommon. Sometimes impatient herders try to sneak into a well, or claim they arrived before another group. Unfortunately, the matter is sometimes, though rarely, settled by brandishing a few of those daggers, and perhaps a gun. Getting your means of survival to its refueling station can be a matter of life and death out there.

****

Truly mesmerized by the scene around us, we knew we were having a special experience. With permission, we took out our camera and snapped a few photos to try and capture what our eyes were witnessing. Most of the people hid their faces.

Offering our thanks for letting us have a glimpse into their lives, we tried to convey to the herders how being there would be a highlight of our time in Africa. They shyly smiled, the way humble people do when positive comments are passed their way.

Looking back over my shoulder, I tried to engrain the scene into my brain. I hoped to never forget it.

(written 5 March 2006)

Life Starts Clapping

We arrived to the office this morning in warm sunshine. When the door to the gate opened, Terefa threw his arms into the air and emoted great joy in seeing us! We shook hands the way Ethiopian men do-a handshake combined with right shoulders knocking and then holding together. The longer you stay in this pose, the happier you are to see the other person.

Terefa held on, and kept saying, "Jim! Jim! Jim!" He smiled bigger than the magical land that is Ethiopia.

Two and half years ago we left Addis, only a few weeks after first meeting Terefa. He was hired as a guard for our office, commonplace for governmental and non-governmental offices in the city. He and I had a few laughs and smiles then, our communication made challenging by language barriers.

Still, he was one of the people I most looked forward to seeing once I was back in Ethiopia.

After the handshake and greeting my wife, he grabbed a hold of me and gave me a big hug. Probably weighing thirty pounds less than me and around twenty or more years my senior, I felt as though I was being bear hugged by a man who goes to the gym several days a week.

"Jim! Jim! Jim!"

"How are you Terefa?"

"Good. I'm good," he said in English.

"You. How are you?"

"I'm happy to see you. Today's a great day!"

"Yes."

Throughout the day whenever I stepped outside, he would call my name, smile on his face and happiness emanating from it. We would laugh, and I'd say his name and we'd laugh some more. What more do two people need to say between them than a smile?

The rain started as we were returning from lunch. Terefa taught us how to say "It's raining now" in Amharic, and we all laughed at my attempt at saying the words. He grabbed me again and put his arms around my shoulders and smiled some more. I knew he loved me.

****

I have another three weeks and some days here. No matter how they play out, seeing Terefa and feeling his love for me is a gift I will carry with me forever. I was surprised by how truly happy he was to see me again. And he taught me a lesson:

To love the people that come into my life, no matter the span of time I am with them or how long we may be apart.

Terefa is a man of little things, but he is a man of big spirit. He is a common man, if you will, but his generous act of welcoming me back was the work of a saint. I feel blessed.

Hafiz has a way of expressing how I feel right now. I'm going to read Life Starts Clapping, a Daniel Ladinsky translation.

(written July 2008)

Berbere Latte

Any coffee enthusiast would find their plane ticket worthwhile upon landing in Addis and walking around town a half-day, visiting some of the local cafes. With names like Sunbird, Red Bean, Kaldi's, Denver, La Parisienne, Skylite, First Cup, and Canada Sol (a few in the Bole area), you'd be in *buna* heaven with the aroma wafting on the air inside.

I'm not much of a coffee drinker, though this time around I have decided to give it a more thorough go on the coffee drinking front. The other afternoon I had a cappuccino at Skylite, and found it easy to drink-ease my way into it with some sweetness.

This morning I had a *berbere* latte. *Berbere* is a smoky pepper spice used in cooking traditional foods, most notably *doro wat* and *tibs*. The former is a delightful chicken stew and the latter is chunks of either goat, lamb, or beef with onions. The *berbere* gives the dishes their distinct Ethiopian flare.

I now understand why coffee can be so addicting; the complexity of the flavor and the buzz combine to make taking a few minutes to appreciate it a meditation of sorts. The latte this morning was a shot of very strong espresso, steamed milk, and *berbere* sprinkled on top. I swirled the pepper spice into the latte. It was deep in flavor, and heavy, or thick maybe, in texture. The spice made the rain extra nice. It would be good in hot chocolate too.

Sipped it a bit, and then I gulped it down while waiting for my veggie pizzas from Pizza Deli Roma, another Italian feature of life in Addis-pizza.

Ethiopians and many Africans show great pride in the fact that Ethiopia is the only African country to never have been colonized. Mussolini was not able to impose a government here. A remnant of that time is the flourishing coffee cafes and pizza shops around the city.

The pizzas arrived a minute or two after I finished the latte. I then started walking back home-a ten minute walk by the Ring Road near the airport. Within a few hundred steps I felt the caffeine kick in.

Wired. Alert.

I stopped by a roadside liquor shack and bought a bottle of local Gouder wine for this evening, and finished my walk home. I opened the gate and went inside, announcing to my wife "berbere latte is my new friend!"

(written July 2008)

Back to Somali-Land

Tomorrow we fly out to Jijiga, a small town on the northern edge of the Ogaden desert in eastern Ethiopia that will serve as base camp for the week. We will be going to two refugee camps to assess our project's efforts there.

I sit here in Addis somewhat excited about the trip; it will be an adventure that is for sure. However, I am also uncertain of what to make of going back after being there for a few days in late 2005.

In the same time frame, I have moved about freely around the globe. And they are still there, having not gone more than a few kilometers from the camp to visit town or gather fuel wood for cooking. For many, they have not seen anything but camp life.

The situation in Somalia has not improved. According to many, it has worsened. The Ethiopian military occupies Mogadishu and other towns, with the support of the United States. Aid workers are being killed. Food aid is not sufficient to feed the people. International organizations/agencies are talking of a massive famine.

And into this reality, is the reality that I will go to refugee camps where Somali people are living so I can monitor a project that truly is working to improve the camp residents' lives. Me. White skin, blue eyes, blond hair-all easily seen on my U.S. passport. Me. Unsupportive of my country's actions in the region. Me. Having to bear the responsibility of owning that passport.

For five days I will be there under the invitation of the UNHCR and the Ethiopian government. I will see abject poverty. I will hear stories that I am not able to imagine as really being true. I will see smiling faces welcoming me into their homes. I will likely hold hands with men in the camp, as is common in this part of the world. I will eat goat, drink spiced tea, and offer whatever hope I can to them when they tell me about wanting to leave.

About wanting to get to Europe. To America. And back to their home villages. I will try to look them in the eye and tell them that it will happen, *Inshallah*. Yet I will know that they know it is near impossible to dream such a dream when you have been living in the camp since 1991.

Tomorrow I travel to Somaliland with a perplexed mind. I'd rather have it this way than be driving to the grocery store and having to decide which bunch of bananas to buy.

(written July 2008)

Two Scenes of Addis

Across from the big, new, Ethiopian Orthodox Church, as you are walking along Cameroon Street away from the airport, is a stately new residential compound. Word is that the second wealthiest man in Ethiopia owns the property.

The parents' home is as opulent as anything you would see in Richville, USA, complete with a hanging chandelier on the one balcony and big open windows so passers-by can see the fine furniture not intended to be sat on and art on the walls. What's more, Dad provided homes for each of his children, four smaller versions, though still several thousand square feet in size, of comfort beyond necessity fall in line along the road.

Video cameras scan the street, guards sit inside little office-like posts by the ornate gates that open to the driveways, and the sidewalk is wide and made from fancy brick. And there are speed bumps along the two-football-field stretch of road that runs in front of the house, a house that could be picked up and transplanted in Beverly Hills and would feel right at home with its neighbors.

****

At the bottom of a small hill on Bole Road, a couple of boys-street kids-wearing dirty, worn clothes, play in the mud puddles of an undeveloped piece of land after a hard rain. They are having a good time, laughing while sliding on their butts in the mud.

Some other boys were washing a minibus that transports people around the city. The driver parked the bus in the runoff, and the boys used the brown water to clean the bus, earning a few Birr for their labor.

By a cinder block wall are little mounds of what appear to be trash, plastic sheets covering whatever might be underneath. That is where they sleep, homeless kids with "homes" on the street.

××*×*×*

If you were to stand inside the parents' house and look out from one of the windows, there is a good chance you could see the boys crawling into their homes at night.

(written July 2008)

Chigryelem

You say it something like this: Chigg-ger-ray-lum, or Chig-grey-lum, or Chigger-ay-lum. Maybe you can roll that "r" in there a bit. Say it fast and let it all blend together, but putting more emphasis on the "chig."

It means "no problem" in Amharic. It is my new favorite word.

If you think Ethiopia is war, famine and disease, too bad for you. Traveling, visiting, and working here is "chigryelem." You quickly learn that Ethiopia is so much more than what the media reports on in the West.

(written August 2008)

Harvesting Teff in Tigray

Acknowledgements

It all begins with my wife, Cheryl. Together, we decided to go, and went, knowing that as long as we had each other, everything else would be fine. It was. In fact, it was more than fine. The gender perspectives in these pages are what I learned from her. Thank you for being patient with me, and for being who you are. Te quiero.

The beginning also includes Harry Stokes, who offered the "job" to us. Job is in quotes, as it never felt like one, at least the way me might define it in the USA. Thank you, Harry, not only for making the offer and sending us but also for sharing your vision, your passion for clean energy, and your genuine concern for people's access to resources and equitable distribution of resources. Not only is what you are doing a household energy revolution, it is also a revolution of thinking and attitudes. You deserve all of the accolades that you have received, which isn't enough.

To the Project Gaia team in Ethiopia and its partners: you inspire me. The commitment and hard work that you exemplify day-after-day is extraordinary, and that is an understatement. The future of Ethiopia is bright due to you. I believe that wholeheartedly.

To the global Project Gaia team, especially in Nigeria and Brazil, thank you for your warmth, smiles, and open arms in welcoming me and sharing your lives with me.

To Dick Young and The Denan Project: what you are doing in Denan seems unbelievable, until you see it. I now believe in the power of steadfastness, stubbornness, tenacity, and humanity's ability to empathize.

To Wanda Murren and Marc Charisse for believing there was a space (literal and figurative) in The Evening Sun for my writings.

To my family back home in McSherrystown, PA: thank you for allowing me to be who I am, which includes each of you. You are with me. Mom and Dad—Thank you for teaching me to care about other people not by saying it, but by living it.

There is no doubt that I am forgetting people. I apologize for that.

Note: some of the photographs in Ethiopian Vignettes: Seeing is Believing were taken by my wife, Cheryl O'Brien.

www.ingramcontent.com/pod-product-compliance
Lightning Source LLC
Chambersburg PA
CBHW020509030426
42337CB00011B/302